Carried Where We Go

poems by
Bart Solarczyk

Copyright © 2022 Bart Solarczyk

All rights reserved. This book or parts thereof may not be reproduced in any form, stored in any retrieval system, or transmitted in any form by any means—electronic, mechanical, photocopy, recording, or otherwise—without prior written permission of the publisher, except as provided by United States of America copyright law. For permission requests, write to the publisher, at "Attention: Permissions Coordinator," at the address below.

Redhawk Publications
The Catawba Valley Community College Press
2550 US Hwy 70 SE
Hickory NC 28602

ISBN: 978-1-952485-86-2

Library of Congress Number:

Printed in the United States of America

redhawkpublications.com

Cover photographs by Bruno Cervera, Nina Simková, and Lex Sirikiat
Cover design by Rosemary Moua

Advance praise for *Carried Where We Go*

"Fantastic book! Bart Solarczyk's on a cosmic Mount Rushmore alongside Brautigan, Bukowski, and Eigner."

—Carter Monroe, author of *Journey*, *The Waffle House Blues*, and *Sittin' in with the Sun*.

"Poet, Bart Solarczyk does the same thing that Larry Brown did in Southern Lit: break the readers' hearts, in his case by holding up his broken heart for them to see, wrestling with, at times even bear-hugging his grief. He does so in poems of astounding economy, a form he has mastered. And yet in *Carried Where We Go*, he manages to balance tragedy with humor, wit, warmth, and the joys of the life he has lived. Solarczyk is the rare poet who gets better every time out. This one may be his best."

—Tim Peeler, author of *The Life of Jesus Christopher Duende*, *Touching All the Bases*, and *First Season*.

"*Carried Where We Go*—the beautiful new collection by Bart Solarczyk—confirms what some of us have known for years: the author is an absolute master. When Charles Bukowski said, 'An artist says a hard thing in a simple way,' he must have been talking about Bart. Very few poets—alive or dead—capture how we spend our days in such perfect language with such amazing insights. Here are poems about stinky old Pittsburgh and broken men speaking truth from bar stools. Here are remembrances of Catholic school that look like flames burning lust into beauty. Beware the crows. The crows are everywhere. Then comes this punch, 'If Santa Claus & Jesus had a baby it wouldn't be me.' Bart Solarczyk is not a saint. He's a genius. A broken genius. He knows love and loss. He knows death. He knows what his wife looks like in heaven. He knows all the ways to remember, and those remembrances will crush your pain and turn it into a diamond ring. He's Johnny Cash writing about June. He's the very best of Richard Brautigan. He's Li Po and he's rock n' roll. If you don't like poetry, pretend Solarczyk is a monk making beer, then drink it down. Different craft, same result—absolute greatness. If you want to feel better about a bad world, read this book. It will set your day on fire in the best way."

—Dave Newman, author of *The Same Dead Songs*

Advance praise for *Carried Where We Go*, continued

"When it comes to brief, short form poetry, Bart Solarczyk is one-of-a-kind, a master of his trade. His work is at once succinct, in-your-face and heartbreakingly lyrical. There are more than a few poets whose work embodies the first two qualities, but unique is the poet who consistently exemplifies all three. *Carried Where We Go* contains some of Solarczyk's best work to date and Redhawk Publications is to be congratulated for making it more generally available to the poetry world."

—Don Wentworth, *Lilliput Review*, editor and publisher emeritus

"Homer once wrote that the gods envy humans because we are mortal, because any moment may be our last and everything is more beautiful because we're doomed. Bart Solarczyk's heartrending and heart-filling new collection, *Carried Where We Go*, sparkles with the beauty that comes with loss. Rich with longing, love, nostalgia, and compassion, these poems simultaneously celebrate and mourn, dance and weep, rage against the dying of the light and find peace in the darkness. There's a lot of raucous joy here, too—Catholic nuns and Baudelaire, beer and pizza, the Blessed Mother in her bathtub shrine bedazzled with immortal plastic flowers, crows and The Three Stooges. Solarczyk—wise, wickedly funny, and tender beyond words—is the poet/guide we need as we move together through this beautiful, temporary, enviable life. I'm so grateful for him."

—Lori Jakiela, author of *How Do You Like It Now, Gentlemen?* and more.

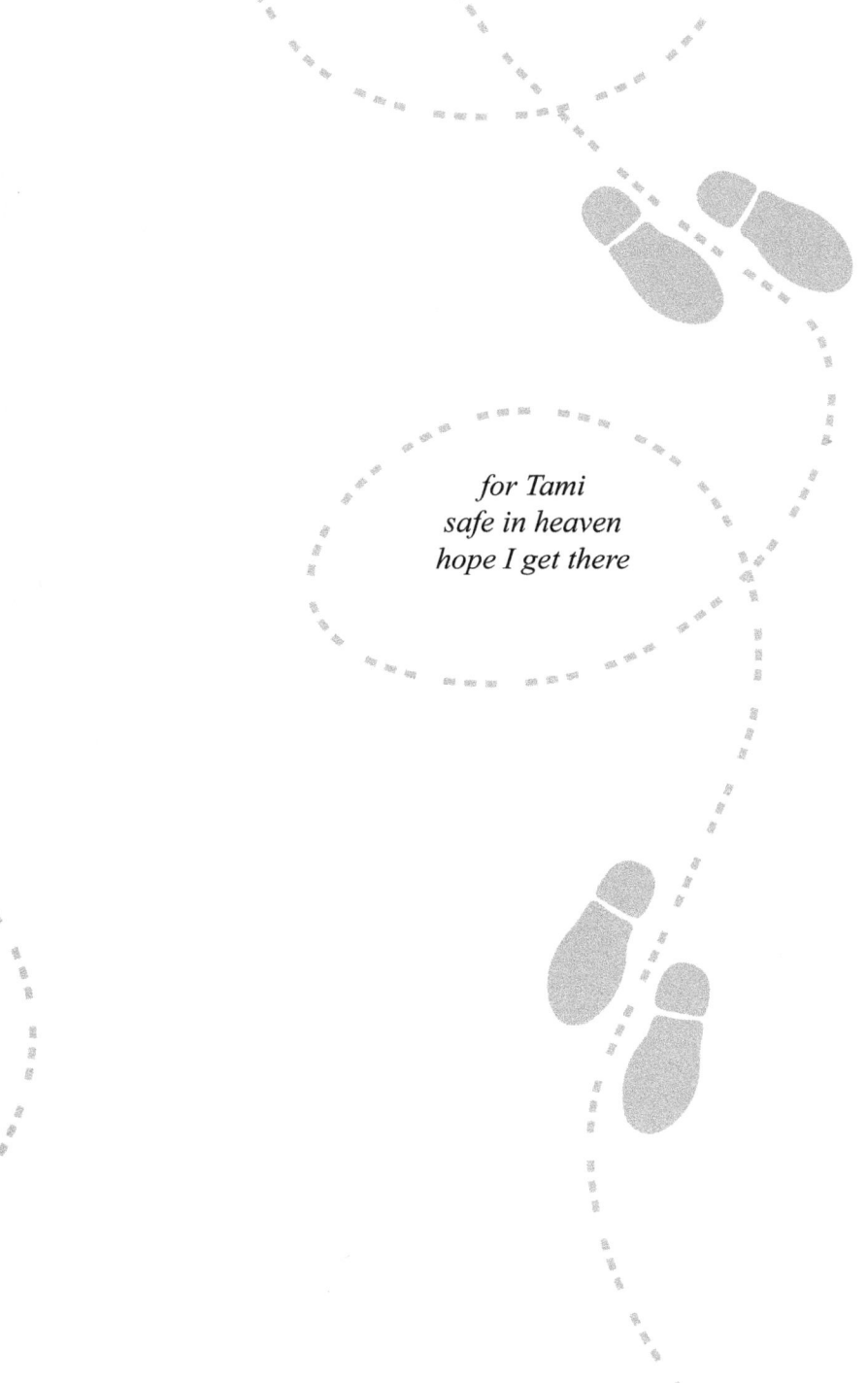

*for Tami
safe in heaven
hope I get there*

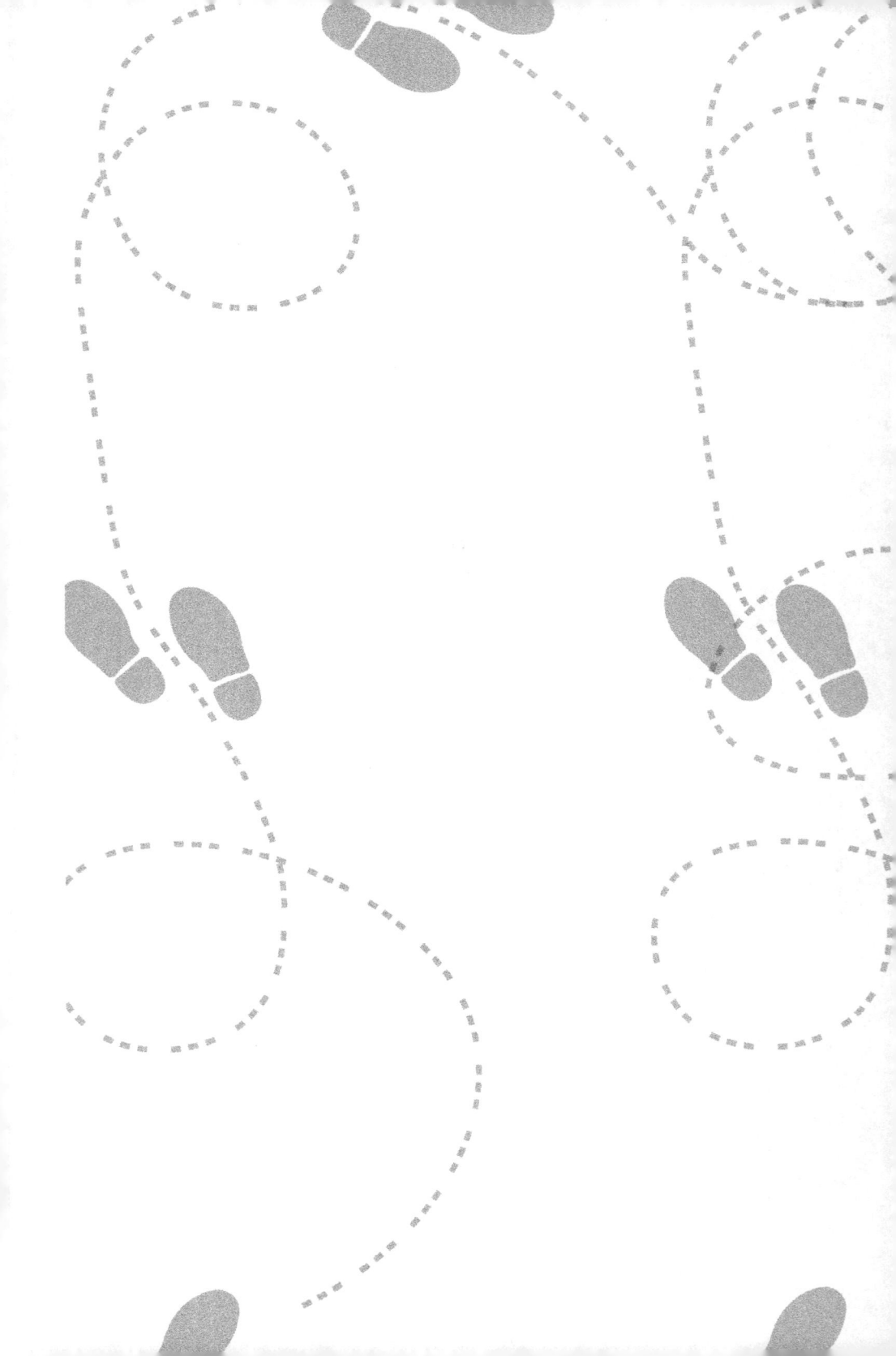

Table of Contents

Third-Hand Clunker	9
Rocket Boys	10
The Zen of Swoose	11
Plastic Flowers	12
Days Without Grace	13
Color My World	14
Hey Catholic Girl	15
Sleepwatching	16
Every Morning	17
5 Short Ones	18
Baudelaire	20
For Deanna	22
A Little Bite of the Dharma	23
For Tami Again Tonight	24
He Goes Out	25
Cool	26
A Dog, a Cat, a Daughter	27
4 Short Ones	28
Bottles & Knives	29
Amelia	30
2 Poems	31
Life in Black & White	32
For Megan Bell	33
Frankenstein	34
2 Crow Poems for Don Wentworth	35
The Three Stooges in Heaven	36
Dear Ron	37
Let's Melt the Cake	38
5 Short Ones	39
Leaning on The Buddha	40
2 holiday haiku	41
Wrapped Too Tight	42
Hog Jowl	43

Carried Where We Go	44
Dusting the Moon	45
Croup	46
Never Really Here	47
6 Short Ones	48
Words & Flowers	49
Myron	50
Purple Hair & Podcasts	51
Three Months Now	52
Fat Thumb on the Scale	53
A Poem for Jyl	54
Why Ask Why	55
drunk haiku	56
Not Yet	57
When I Know	58
Now You're Everywhere	59
Some Days	60
riverdog haiku	61
10/20/20	62
Tami	63
Stunned in Blue Light	64
Shadow People	65
Crow Heart	66
Squatting With The Buddha	67
Gray to White	68
Light Peeks Out	69
6 Short Ones	70
The Poems Will Save Me	71
Empty Hands	72
The Color of Absence	73
I Circle Back	74
The Crow's Disappointment	75
Those Simple Yesterdays	76
Meet the Drunken Axe	77
No Feathered Oracle	78
My Friend the Crow	79
4 Short Ones	80
Acknowledgments	82

Bart Solarczyk

Third-Hand Clunker

The mill smells like egg farts
& the slaughterhouse like
ten-thousand brutal deaths

we're riding somewhere fun
in dad's latest
used used car

mom gags
as we pinch noses
in the backseat

windows cranked
we bake
until safe wind

summer in Pittsburgh
hot & stinky
to be that boy again

bad air
a third-hand clunker
& everyone still here.

Rocket Boys

Shadow blood in black & white
we walk it backwards to when
shit made a difference
& ghosts hung on the line
all dirty gray

uncles drunk on porches
tossing cousins
we took turns
laughing rocket boys
arced between heroes.

Bart Solarczyk

The Zen of Swoose

The quick & the maimed & the road kill
pigeons dreaming on a roof
& the drunks screwed to their stools

someday son all this can be yours
he was a sad & honest man
I believed him, it came to be.

Plastic Flowers

Queen of city steps & soot
Blessed Mother
in a bathtub shrine

embracing slag, smoke & hammers
come adore her
plastic flowers never die.

Bart Solarczyk

Days Without Grace

In church, in the parking lot
the crows are hopping mad
& then they swirl against the gray air
grim as a ninety-year-old virgin
swirl like black beads in a rosary
made of cancer.
   *

Jimmy P pissed himself while kneeling upright, he had his
hand raised but Sister Spetzciosa didn't see it so he pissed
his pants too fearful to leave Mass without permission, he
was trembling, crying in a sweater stretched with holes, it
was winter, when we got back to class Sister had him stand
facing the hissing radiator in the back of the room until he
dried enough to sit at his sad desk where he got slapped
because he wouldn't stop crying

Color My World

(for Suzanne P)

We danced with
nuns watching

keep your distance
move your hands

guarding the dark places
where we might disappear

color my world
stay in my corner

only love can
break your heart

didn't I blow your mind
this time & more

walking home
to different lives

we touched
but never kissed

kept walking to
where we are right now.

Bart Solarczyk

Hey Catholic Girl

St. Francis hugged a leper
to overcome his fear

I'm not that scabby
let's help each other heal

joined as believers
in the word made flesh

this blessed sacrament
that brings what we confess.

Sleepwatching

The veins run smooth
& blue
beneath her pale flesh.
Makes me want to kiss
her hands,
kiss the pretty pipes
that pump her blood.
Love cultivates
peculiar whims,
cultivates such cravings.
Love can stare for hours
& never blink.
She smiles in her sleep,
shifts
& smacks her lips.
She smiles in her sleep
& dreams I'm watching.

Every Morning

How sweet
to have a lover
who brings it
every morning

& how sad
to know so early
the best part of the day
is already gone.

5 Short Ones

hot morning piss
I bless my enemies
the memories of their failures

sun, wind, rain
we're still here
us & the rocks

moonflower blossoms
like a bruise
across November sky

for what it costs
to feed a dog
I could be rid of you

if Santa Claus & Jesus
had a baby
it wouldn't be me

◇◇ Bart Solarczyk

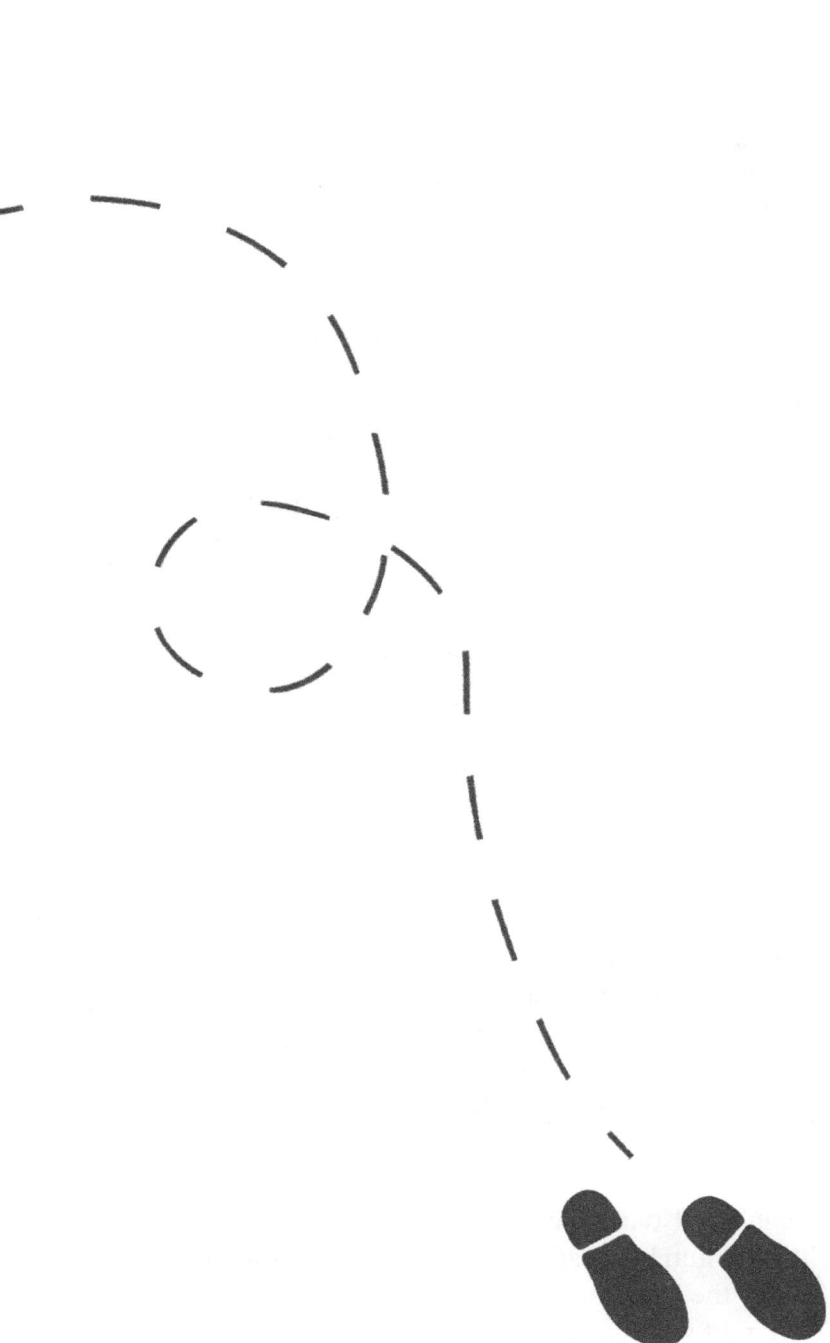

Baudelaire

Baudelaire ate opium
Baudelaire loved wine & smoked hashish
Baudelaire celebrated the company of whores
Baudelaire wrote beautiful poems
but spent his money badly

If Baudelaire was around today
I'd invite him over to the house
I'd crack him a longnecked Rolling Rock
& offer him my pipe
I'd say: "You're not such a bad guy, Charlie.
I think I can see where you're pinned."

I'd send the wife out shopping
then call for a pizza & an escort service.
Pay for it all with my Mastercard

We'd drink & sing & debauch
while the neighbors hid & prayed
behind drawn curtains

After the whores had robbed us
we'd write a poem
& post it on the internet.
Then we'd smoke a few bowls in the backyard
while shadows ate the sun.
We'd listen to evening birdsongs
& watch for the first star.

Eventually I'd call a cab for Baudelaire
I'd hand him his chapeau & guide his drunk ass to the door
I'd pay the driver
We'd part without a word

Bart Solarczyk

I'd stagger up the porch steps
lock up & count myself lucky

I mean Baudelaire's alright
but I don't need him
crashing on my sofa.

For Deanna

some mornings shimmer golden—
red hair framing flesh
in last night's dream

Bart Solarczyk

A Little Bite of the Dharma

Bugs on Buddha's bunghole
it's all Jack's itchy dream

so scratch your ass or not
it's the same thing.

For Tami Again Tonight

The decades spin
I suck your toes
you giggle & talk dirty

make another wish
those sparks are stars
& love's pushed luck this far.

Bart Solarczyk

He Goes Out

He goes out drunk
& comes home drunk
then writes a poem
about going out
& coming home drunk

it gets published
in a small magazine
or more likely online
then he goes out
& comes home drunk again.

Cool

(for Meghan Tutolo)

I saw her on her scooter
parked behind the Walmart
watching the sunset
while eating Honey Grahams

& I knew all at once
this was love
I knew all at once this was
everything always
I knew she was my bouncy girl
chewing through a smile

she's so cool
she makes cool look overrated.

A Dog, a Cat, a Daughter

Home after the music
& a twelve-pack

he breaks bread
like a peasant

thinks of Christ
& bows his head

the wife watching TV
a dog, a cat, a daughter

giving thanks should
always come so easy.

4 Short Ones

snow on gray mountains
this is my life now
why not smile?

cricket on the hearth
mother sends me out
to play her number

seven moons
bring a week's
worth of wine

our parrot
sweet talks my wife
in another man's voice

Bottles & Knives

You can kill with bottles & knives
or just get drunk
& cut the pizza

you can stand against the world
like a prophet
at the gate

or post a poem in seven groups
that garners
forty-nine likes

the best minds
of my generation
simpering.

Amelia

Barefoot dancer
wounded healer
mother, lover, friend

joy flies on thin wings
but still arrives

fierce against foul winds
& broken light
breath turns sweet

all pixie sparkle
& laughing gypsy eyes.

Bart Solarczyk

2 Poems

in the mirror
I am dog
obey me

creepy old man
brushing his teeth
in my mirror

Life in Black & White

There's this story where
the pretty girls hitchhike

while the glue sniffers
circle in their trucks

a kerosene landscape
with cheap beer seats

& every hole in every head
bleeding shadows.

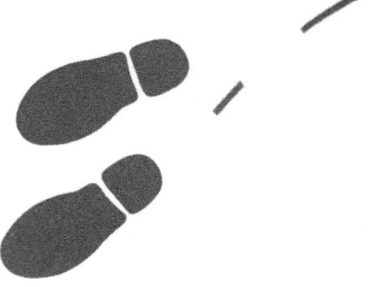

Bart Solarczyk

For Megan Bell

bruised, pierced, painted
life is skin
save room for me

Frankenstein

Beer good
beer my friend

drinking beer
with the monster

a patchwork
with few words

but he makes
a lot of sense.

Bart Solarczyk

2 Crow Poems for Don Wentworth

Old man crow
in the bleachers
remembers when
the Pirates were good

Pittsburgh crow
knows a jagoff
when he sees one

The Three Stooges in Heaven

Moe doesn't look like Hitler
& Larry's downright handsome

Curly spins on a cloud
nyuk, nyuk, nyuk

there is no Shemp.

Bart Solarczyk

Dear Ron

So far it's six beers
& six Sicilian slices

could get better if you
float me six green clouds.

Let's Melt the Cake

(for Tami on my birthday)

Sixty-one years
of fuck-ups & failures

& more than half that time
you've spent squished against my heart

so fire up all those candles
then wiggle over here

let's melt the cake
let's make that sugar burn.

5 Short Ones

from a baby
to a lonely old man—
who blinked?

loud, beautiful, mean
blue jay bully
trumpets his arrival

tangerine
you could be
next week's moon

before the day
turns hard
the cat's orange head

nail guns & men
shouting in Spanish—
my neighbor's new roof

Leaning on The Buddha

(for DS)

The first time I meet Dan
he says it's a good day
to die in the streets

how many friendships
have been built
upon less?

Bart Solarczyk

2 holiday haiku

save the box
the bow—
bad beer gets regifted

auld lang syne
resolutions—
vomit in a rusty tub

Wrapped Too Tight

I should smash my face
against this table

I should smash my face
against your face

Merry Christmas
in an angry world motherfucker

Merry Christmas
it's such an angry world.

Bart Solarczyk

Hog Jowl

(for Meghan T)

Pig in a poke
bacon in a bag
hog jowl in the White House

we are what we've become
or something like that.

Carried Where We Go

(for Megan at The Coffee Buddha)

Beauty blossoms new each day
if we fix our eyes to see it

wisdom comes with age
if we keep the door ajar

there will be pain, there will be loss
what we hold will shatter

but hearts bind in the dark
love follows light

friends are folks we didn't know
who arrive unexpected

& never leave
carried where we go.

Bart Solarczyk

Dusting the Moon

Dusting the moon
with drunken wishes

as gravity
folds our wings

falling through
last call

with nothing
granted.

Croup

A lie needs a liar
& someone to believe it

drugs need pain
& broken teeth a smile

the sound of poets crackling
blue smoke swirling glass

the croup of failure
the necessity of lungs

Never Really Here

We fortify
we fade
we transition

never really here
the last
of our kind.

6 Short Ones

in the room where
the blood & skin landed
the janitor's boots

flayed
by the absence of dreams
but only when I sleep

old man multitasking
writing haiku in my head
while walking Pittie

red hawk on the swing set
knows there's murder in the air
crows, always fucking crows

an ocean between us
& still I get lost
in your eyes

the stars are late
& so am I
Alicia's waiting

Words & Flowers

We greet death
with words & flowers

then go home
& make believe we don't.

Myron

The sorrow of an orange cat
who isn't what he was

thin sack of bones
now memory & ash.

Bart Solarczyk

Purple Hair & Podcasts

(for Ne'Cole)

Pain shapes our paths
in ways
we'd rather not walk

yet we arrive
voices breaking air
still sexy.

Three Months Now

The side of my neighbor's house
looks like a yellow brick skull
with a green hedge beard
& dirty window eyes

it watches past the driveway
watches me drink backyard beer
watches while I kiss the silver pipe

watches like it knows something
I don't but I do
gone three months now
she's not coming back.

Bart Solarczyk

Fat Thumb on the Scale

The weight of feathered dreams
a man's weight in ashes

lost between the numbers
there's a life.

A Poem for Jyl

Imagine flowers with a smile
hope on feathered wings
words from my tablet
to your table

the miracle of skin
in such uncertain times
where the wounded come
to love again
& strangers can be friends

steam rises from warm cups
birds sing our favorite songs
may this day be as beautiful
as you are.

Bart Solarczyk

Why Ask Why

when we both know
dust to dust
et cetera

once stars
now this

accept it.

drunk haiku

he drinks—
flowers
bend to rain

more reason to weep—
drunk
without a dog

this winter whiskey path—
my eyes
two pissholes in the snow

I lie when
I drink—
I'm not drinking

Bart Solarczyk

Not Yet

Every time it knocks
I stall & say not yet

but it keeps knocking
not yet, please not yet.

When I Know

Why would I want
to go back
when I know

I never was
the man
I used to be.

Bart Solarczyk

Now You're Everywhere

There's a dark spot on the floor
of the upstairs hallway where you died

it won't bleach out
it wants me to remember

as if I needed death's stain
on worn hardwood to remind me

now you're everywhere
but I'm not, please find me.

Some Days

Some days thirst
comes early

some days
I succumb

some days wobble
more than others.

Bart Solarczyk

riverdog haiku

Rae's crows caw & cackle
counting sorrows
four children & no fathers

Tami I'm so lost
I don't even
dream you anymore

sharp & sudden
everything
you miss

her princess dreams
& rag doll dress
come morning

streetlight stretches shadows
dog, me
devil on my shoulder

10/20/20

Rain's blue gloom
I'm quarantined
with dreams
on life support
disguised as poems.

Bart Solarczyk

Tami

Every inch a mile
& every clock eternity

I miss you, I stay drunk
I'm on my way.

Stunned in Blue Light

Naked, dead & dumped
on the roadway
rolls so easy from
the anchorman's tongue

you're smoking dope
& nine beers in
the dog sleeping on the sofa
stunned in blue light
& reaching for the fridge

you like your numbers even
the balance it brings

she was somebody's
something
or maybe not
& that makes it worse.

Shadow People

Shadow people
try to suck my breath
but I win again

I keep winning
until the day
I don't.

Crow Heart

In the rain on the wire
on the cold bare branch
shadow in the autumn sky

crow sees me drunk
caws my name like a curse
crow heart lonely like mine.

Squatting With The Buddha

The earth eats shit
& turns it into flowers.

Gray to White

The small things become big
in both the doing & the meaning

years so long once now gone fast
you're here & you're this old

the small things become big
layered like lost smiles

the doing & the meaning
gray to white, ashes in a jar.

Light Peeks Out

(for Alicia M)

Blue Alicia
ever beautiful
even when she's sad

poems & pain & pictures
windowed heart
light peeks out, love breaks in.

6 Short Ones

numbering absence
all the ways
I miss you

dog in the sun
I'm here too
not who I was

blue lonely sea
but the sky
remains kind

motorcycle
summer bus
cicadas

the memories
we don't remember
are frequently the best

dark water moon
pour me a poem
& watch me sink

The Poems Will Save Me

The poems will save me
the words will lift
my head above grief

but how to believe
the poems will save me
when it's all so sad?

Empty Hands

I dream you naked in a world
where touch is forbidden

this is death, this is longing
empty hands squeezing air.

The Color of Absence

The color of passion
the color of blood
the color of penance

the color of iron
when malleable

the color of a bruise
that's almost pretty

the color of absence

the color of wings
clipped too young

the color of dreams
where we touch
& you're still here

impossible color.

I Circle Back

Memories lie like
scat in melting snow

the trick is getting home
with clean boots.

The Crow's Disappointment

A bruise in the wind
the crow's disappointment
mother's husk fixed
pretty in her bed

beer rings on the table
ashes on the floor
a calendar of days
before the plague

the caw of judgment
the essence of subtraction
to live with less
to carry all that's gone

the wisdom in a gut pile
the refuse of our dreams
the next first step
the dread beneath dark wings.

Those Simple Yesterdays

I dream you entering the room
smiling with a sandwich

all those simple yesterdays
believing there would always
be tomorrow.

Meet the Drunken Axe

Would you live another life
would you give this one back
to face the blade & hope
the next one will be better?

Empty hands shape idle plans
Mr. Wetbrain late night reverie
meet the drunken axe then
rise again sharp & polished.

No Feathered Oracle

Tami I'm all ears
but you're still keeping secrets
two years gone

no message in the clouds
no feathered oracle
blue sky is just blue sky.

My Friend the Crow

Mortality, a fisted heart
the drag of loneliness

& my friend the crow
swallowing your name.

4 Short Ones

autumn crow
hops & laughs
hops & laughs

tune in a bucket
swinging
in the afterglow

going back
to say goodbye
tomorrow

blue world
in the backyard
blue me

Bart Solarczyk

Acknowledgments

Grateful acknowledgment is made to the editors of the following zines, journals, newspapers, or websites where some of these poems in this book first appeared:

Alien Buddha Zine, Be About It Zine, Big Hammer, Duane's PoeTree, Issa's Untidy Hut, Lilliput Review, Live Nude Poems, Nixes Mate Review, Paper Boat Haiku Revue, The Pittsburgh Book Review, Pittsburgh Magazine, The Pittsburgh Post-Gazette, Poem A Day: The Shaler North Hills Library Website, Rasputin, Riverdog, Roadside Raven Review, Street Value, Trailer Park Quarterly, Wine-drunk Sidewalk, Yawp.

"Sleepwatching" was published in the chapbook, *The Place of Broken Arrows* (kali momma press, 1994).

"Baudelaire" was published in the chapbook, *Vicodin & The Christian Broadcasting Network* (fingerprintpress, 2004).

"Sleepwatching," "Let's Melt the Cake," & "For Tami Again Tonight" appeared in *Unconditional Surrender: An Anthology of Love Poems* (Low Ghost Press, 2017).

Special thanks to Scott Silsbe for his assistance in typing, editing, & assembling this manuscript.

 Bart Solarczyk is a lifelong resident of Pittsburgh, PA. Over the past forty years his poems have been published in print & online in a variety of magazines, journals, anthologies, broadsides & chapbooks. He is the author of two full-length poetry collections: *Tilted World* (Low Ghost Press) & *Classic Chapbooks* (Redhawk Publications).

www.ingramcontent.com/pod-product-compliance
Lightning Source LLC
Chambersburg PA
CBHW031208090426
42736CB00009B/839